SIDE SADDLE RIDING

SIDE SADDLE RIDING

NOTES FOR TEACHERS AND PUPILS

BETTY SKELTON

· THE ·
SPORTSMAN'S
PRESS
LONDON

Published by The Sportsman's Press, 1988

© Betty Skelton 1988

All rights reserved. No part of this publication may be reproduced, stored in a retrieval system, or transmitted in any form or by any means, electronic, mechanical, photocopying, recording or otherwise, without the prior permission of the publishers.

British Library Cataloguing in Publication Data

Skelton, E.C. (Elizabeth Clare), *1909*-
 Side saddle riding : notes for
 teachers and pupils.
 1. Livestock : Horses. Side-saddle riding -
 Manuals
 I. Title
 798.2'3

ISBN 0-948253-24-X

Printed in Great Britain by
Adlard & Son Ltd, Dorking, Surrey

CONTENTS

List of Plates   7

1 Introduction   9

2 The Beginner   12
Helping the pupil obtain a comfortable seat – exercises to encourage the correct riding position – the position of the hands

3 Improving the Rider   19
The rider's hands – reins and bridles – the rising trot – lunging for the side saddle rider – teaching jumping

4 Clothes and Tradition   30
A brief history of clothing for side saddle riding – the Side Saddle Association's guide to correct turn out

5 Saddlery   34
The development of the modern side saddle – a guide to purchasing for the new side saddle rider – girths – stirrup – sticks – bridles – saddling up

6 Choice of Horse for Side Saddle   42
The main factors in the horse's conformation – advice to the beginner

7 Advice to Instructors   44
The role of the Instructor today

8 Side Saddle Instructor's Examination and Tests   48
Qualifications for Instructors – Side Saddle Association's proficiency tests for the side saddle rider – Association of British Riding Schools' tests covering equitation and stable management

9 The Revival of Side Saddle in England and America   53

Bibliography   59

LIST OF PLATES

1 Mounting

2 Correct position of the legs
  Good position of the hands

3 Mrs Barham, Vice-President of the Side Saddle Association
  Correct dress for a Hack Class at small shows

4 Mayhew, Owen and Champion & Wilton saddles

5 Offside of Mayhew saddle showing outside girths
  Offside girth straps of Owen and Champion & Wilton

6 A selection of girths
  Mayhew saddle showing balance strap

7 Mayhew, Owen and Champion & Wilton safety stirrup bars

8 Turning in mid air when jumping off against the clock
  Mrs Barham's first Display Team

1
INTRODUCTION

Recently I was in London with a friend from America searching for more information about side saddle and for books on the subject. We went to see my old friend, Mr Allen, who has so often over the years given so generously of his time and knowledge in helping me to find the books that I have wanted to read. At the end of our conversation it was decided that after having taught side saddle for over half a century I really should get down to writing a book about it.

What background do I come from and how did I gain the experience and knowledge I have to pass on to the new generation of side saddle riders? When I first rode side saddle it was because of convention – nowadays the side saddle rider does so out of choice, convention does not enter into it.

As a teenager in the 1920s, side saddle riding was second nature to me. I found it comfortable and I did not fall off as often as I had done from a cross saddle. I had ridden as a child and had progressed from a donkey to a wilful Exmoor pony through to a half Thoroughbred pony which I found more biddable. In those days everyone rode or drove to where they wanted to go, out to tea or lunch with relatives or friends, and our ponies and horses were our only means of transport.

We, that was my brother, three cousins and I, hunted with the family pack of hounds, the Ashford Valley. I first remember them as a harrier pack, later as foxhounds. As a child I had the usual and probably more than the usual amount of falls, since I was the youngest of the five cousins and we all rode together, and in trying to keep up with them I was always parting company from my pony. Following my parents' divorce my riding came to an abrupt end.

When my maternal grandmother, with whom I went to live, allowed me to hunt again with my father I was put on a side saddle. I was never actually taught to ride side saddle – I just rode out with our old groom on the Thursday. The elastic of my apron was put over my foot, we rode out of the yard, and then walked, trotted and cantered during the ride. Of course I had seen my mother, aunts and members of the family hunt riding side saddle. The following day I was put on a show jumper and she took me over a course of show jumps – my father saying something to the effect that since I was going to hunt the next day I'd better jump a fence or two. My father, whom I adored, was fearless where horses were concerned so he would not have understood if had I said that I was frightened, which I was! But my little short-tailed black horse pranced under me and took me round the show jumps and I was amazed to find that I was still sitting there feeling happy and surprised at being at Goldwell, my Grandfather's home again, with hounds in the kennels, terriers running around and tomorrow I was to hunt. I was back with my father and life was good. And so I hunted all the rest of that season, and for a further two seasons. But then our hounds were sold and my father went to hunt the Llangibby pack. I then rode with the Shorncliffe Drag Hounds whilst working part-time as a secretary before going out to India, with my side saddles, to marry my husband who was in the Army.

When we returned to England I started showing other peoples' horses side saddle. I did not have a horse of my own – but in addition to showing, I taught and schooled horses at the local riding schools where we were stationed – and I would show friends how to sit on a side saddle to enable them to show their own horses in Ladies' classes. In those days I had yet to discover how to teach side saddle; in fact my first side saddle pupil was Peggy Cowey who later became my daughter's godmother for, as with so many of my pupils, we had become friends.

In the course of developing my own method of teaching side saddle, I have discovered and invented suitable exercises to help the rider's position. On becoming Vice-President and then President of the Ladies' Side Saddle Association I felt I should really try to learn more of the science of side saddle riding in order to be more helpful to members of the Association wishing to enhance their skills in side saddle riding. This made me become even more interested in the subject, from saddles, to riders and the schooling of horses to carry a side saddle.

INTRODUCTION

I think that before this time I had just sat on horses in happy ignorance and enjoyed my riding and hunting. Hunting and riding were one and the same thing to me and it was all fun; it was an escape from life and its attendant nuisances – of all the things one ought to do – and we could forget all the worries we had in the sheer enjoyment of being with hounds, jumping fences and galloping and all on a side saddle. Therefore I now offer my ideas developed over the years from my experiences of teaching people to enjoy the safety and security of side saddle riding – from children to a pupil who at the age of 64 had never ridden before and in three months was showing horses and thoroughly enjoying it. It is unlikely that this could have been achieved on a cross saddle.

There are many roads to the same destination, and whilst I do not always agree with everything I read in books on the subject I still recommend these books to my pupils as books and reading will broaden their outlook. We do not all think alike and I do not expect everybody to agree with me, but in order to move with the times improvement is necessary. In 1942 Santini wrote that the lack of interest in side saddle was 'due to poor instruction'; let us, in order to move forwards, now try to share our knowledge and improve our instruction and understanding.

2
THE BEGINNER

The first thing to do with the pupil who has decided she is interested in side saddle is to let her 'have a go' and find out if she likes it. It is best for her either to find someone who teaches side saddle or a friend who has a quiet horse and is willing to let her ride, preferably on the lunge. The idea is to let the rider get an idea of what it feels like to sit on a side saddle with a horse moving under her. It is essential to have a quiet horse and better to have one with a very smooth trot and canter.

Give the rider a leg up so that she is sitting astride her saddle. She should sit squarely with her shoulders facing forward. Place her left hand on the top pommel and her right hand on the balance strap. Then ask her to swing her right leg over and place it hanging down the horse's left shoulder, allowing the width of two fingers between the bend of the knee joint and the top pommel. The right hand should not move. Now place the left leg comfortably against the saddle, leaving a hand's thickness between the rider's left thigh and the leaping head with the knee against the saddle. Here it should be explained that, when riding side saddle, the left knee supports the rider upward on top of the saddle (this is the complete opposite of the present day teaching of knee out of the saddle, calf on the saddle, as in astride riding). This upward support helps the rider to sit on top of her saddle while a pendulous left leg would merely drag the rider's weight down to the left of the saddle.

The rider should sit lightly on her left seat bone thereby distributing the weight towards the right to compensate for the weight of two legs on the left. Some say the rider should imagine she has a drawing pin under her left seat bone. In Germany they liken it to sitting on a raw egg which must not be broken! Care should be taken not to overdo this otherwise the rider will lean to the right which is incorrect. The rider should think of carrying her weight on her right seat bone and along her right thigh until she finds the point of balance which is where the right leg crosses the horse's spine. This is where the hands will naturally fall. This can be tested by raising the hands sideways, allowing them to fall to the side and then lifting them into the lap. The elbows will be bent in the correct position of 'arms close to the sides'.

When the pupil is comfortably seated, the two legs being on the left side of the horse, the rider places her right hand on the balance strap and the left hand on the top pommel. The instructor now walks the horse to the right. This helps the rider to keep her weight up onto the saddle. Then try a slow trot, but do not dwell too long on the trot, move to a slow canter which is the most comfortable pace for the side saddle rider. Should the rider never have ridden a horse before then the Instructor should be cautious and know the horse that she is going to lunge the pupil on. But with a well-trained horse, used to working side saddle, the beginner should be able to walk, trot and canter within ten minutes unless the rider tenses her body because she is nervous. Then confidence must be gained before introducing a few strides of canter.

The position of the rider in the saddle is very important. The rider must sit straight, her shoulders square with the horse's shoulders. The following suggestions may help the beginner. While standing on the ground put the right leg over the left leg, remembering to keep the shoulders square to the front so that you feel a slight twist from waist to hips. This feeling of being crooked and yet knowing that your shoulders still face in the right direction is the whole secret of side saddle riding. The besetting fault of most side saddle riders is to allow the right shoulder to fall forward which it will naturally do to follow the direction of the right leg over to the left. With two legs on the left side the rest of the body weight has to be directed towards the right so that the rider presents a picture sitting squarely on the horse. This is achieved by concentrating on getting the weight along the right thigh and into the right seat bone.

It is interesting to see how secure most riders feel. Some years ago I was asked to give a demonstration to a riding club. I invited one or two of the audience to come forward and have a ride, preferably those who had never ridden before. (I had brought a very experienced and gentle side saddle mare with me, who I knew I could trust). A young girl of about fifteen came forward. I put her into the saddle as described. I asked her if she felt comfortable at both the walk and the trot and then I put the mare into her rocking horse canter, all within three minutes. Someone in the audience said I was lucky, the rider was a natural. So I asked for a second rider and repeated the performance. I know that this would be impossible to do with an astride saddle, and it thus proves the claim that the side saddle gives a much greater feeling of security. The pommels support the rider's legs and the hands keep the body in the correct position. The rider will either immediately express pleasure, or if she doesn't it is unlikely that she will every enjoy riding side saddle.

It should be understood that a rider can ride either side of a horse. That is why someone who has become disabled by an accident can find that riding on the offside suits her better than the nearside, according to which leg has been damaged. Riding with the two legs on the near side of the horse has become the recognised way of riding side saddle but there are offside saddles to be found as well as reversible ones. In my younger days my mother rode on alternate sides every other day and woe betide the groom who forgot which side it was to be on any particular day!

The beginner's position, as described above, is a step towards riding side saddle. However the rider will find that her muscles quickly begin to ache and she should rest frequently, putting her right leg back over the right side of the saddle, lowering the toes, and circling the feet to relax the muscles of the legs.

It is a good idea to start exercises to encourage the rider to transfer her weight onto the right seat bone and along the right thigh. First work at the walk, trot and then at the canter. These exercises are best carried out on the lunge; in a class lesson the left hand has to hold the reins.

Exercise 1 While the left hand remains on the pommel the rider swings the right arm forward, upward and backward slowly, and watches the hand with her eyes, thus moving the head and shoulder to follow the movement. This supples the waist as well as moving the weight into the right seat bone.

Exercise 2 The rider places her right hand behind her back, raising it as high as possible. This corrects a tendency for rounding the right shoulder forward and holds a steady position, whereas the swinging arm rotates the body more. This exercise merely holds the rider in a good position. The higher the arm the better.

Exercise 3 Raise both arms and turn the body to the right so bringing the weight onto the right seat bone and into the right thigh. This movement, as well as bringing the left knee into the supporting position, also keeps the right leg pressed against the safe of the saddle. These exercises look very elegant when performed rhythmically with the horse. Ideally the Instructor should have someone else to lunge the horse so that he or she can stand outside the lunge circle and watch both sides of the rider so as to keep a check on the position of the legs and body.

Exercise 4 For those riders who are inclined to raise the right knee off the saddle and show daylight between the saddle and their right knee: whilst on the lunge rein raise the left hand above the head and, placing the right hand on the balance strap now swing the left hand over to touch the girth or the bottom of the right hand saddle flap. If not on the lunge rein, then take the reins in the right hand just enough to guide and steady the horse. This exercise can be easily adapted for the forward/ jumping position: place the rider's hands on the horse's mane or neck strap and with both hands in this position the rider shifts the weight onto the right thigh, thus lifting the weight off the rider's seat bones – and arrives at the correct jumping position. But for practising this position, when first learning to jump, it is better, on the lunge, to take the left hand forward to hold the mane and put the right hand back to the balance strap. This keeps the right shoulder back in a good position.

Exercise 5 Many side saddle riders do not hold their bodies upright enough and so lose a lot of elegance; this exercise is to straighten the back and lift the diaphragm. Lift both hands above the head and straighten the back, then lower the hands, the right one to the balance strap and the left one to the top pommel. This is the same as the cross saddle exercise of raising the hands above the head, only the side saddle rider must think of making herself taller.

Exercise 6 This exercise aims to supple the shoulders and encourage the back to absorb the horse's movement without rocking. Roll the shoulders around and backwards and forwards.

Exercise 7 This is an exercise for the correct position of the head and to stop the chin poking forward, and is really a continuation of the previous exercise. I have always thought of these two exercises as being the French exercises as I connect the French with suppleness and elegance. I have also, for many years, used these exercises for cross saddle riders as well. Roll the head in a circular movement in both directions so as to stretch the neck as much as possible. Now think of the French who say that the neck is a continuation of the spine and that the head sits on top of the spine. It is amazing to see how fast all riders improve their head carriage with this exercise.

It should be explained to the rider that the stirrup is used only as a footrest – not as in cross saddle where the weight is sunk down into the stirrup. I advocate that a stirrup should not be used to start with, particularly with a pupil who has previously ridden cross saddle as she may be tempted to put her weight into the one stirrup and thus pull herself off the top of the saddle towards the left, which is a very common fault. It may be found sometimes that a heavy or tall lady requires more support than she can obtain from her left knee only. In such a case a stirrup may help the rider to balance herself on top of the saddle, but keep a gap just wide enough for a hand to be slipped between her left thigh and the leaping head. Gripping upwards into the leaping head must be avoided.

When the rider is on the lunge, and not using reins, the position of the body can be held correctly by the position of the hands on the saddle. However, an Instructor may often be faced with a class of beginners for whom lunging is impossible through lack of suitable horses or because of the time factor. In such cases riders will not have the advantages of the introduction to side saddle as described above and the question of controlling the horse whilst keeping a good position will prove more difficult, for it will be found that the position of the hands is of critical importance to the correct position of the rider in the side saddle.

The Position of the Hands It should be stressed that the side saddle rider is sitting a foot further back on her horse than when riding cross saddle and that her hands are therefore further back. It will be found that the over-all length of ordinary reins, i.e., about 1.37 m (54 ins), is too short to allow much movement of the hands. So the lady's reins should be 1.68m (66 ins) overall instead of the usual length. When off the lunge the rider has to contend with the control of the horse and her body. If the horses are easy to control then the riders are asked to ride with two reins in the left hand and to put the right hand onto the balance strap to keep the shoulders square with the horse's shoulders. It will however often be found that the horses present at the lesson are not used to working together in an enclosed area such as an all-weather arena or a covered school. So problems can arise and one realises the worth of private lessons with the use of a lunge rein and good school horses used to working correctly with a side saddle.

Should the rider not have side saddle length reins, then put a piece of plaiting thread through the end of the rein and tie a piece of string from that to the buckle of the rein. Better still, have a length of rein made with the billet and buckle which can be fastened on to the cross saddle reins when riding side saddle. Best of all, have a pair of reins made especially for side saddle riding; they will not be found to be uncomfortably long for cross saddle riding.

A practical way to get the right position of the hands is to let the riders sit astride their saddles, raise their arms sideways and let their hands fall into their saddles just in front of them. Thus it will be found that the hands fall behind the top pommel. This is the natural and correct position into which the hands will fall. In this way the urge to put the hands into the usual position when riding cross saddle – i.e., in front of the right knee – will be corrected before it has begun. If the wrong position (which one sees all too often) is uncorrected the shoulders and the whole body are dragged forward, thus depriving the rider of the use of her back and seat bones which are the most important aids for the side saddle rider.

Having discussed the position of the hands when teaching a class of beginners, and hoping that most of the horses are quiet and sensible, riders can now take up the side saddle position with their right legs over the top pommel and the reins in their left hand, keeping the right hand on the balance strap, if possible, so as to ensure that their right elbow stays over the line of the right hip. Then walk the horses forward on the right rein (it may be found that some riders will need two hands to control their horses). If possible, the reins being long enough, the rider can keep the right hand towards the balance strap. Then each individual in turn should trot until she joins the rear of the ride, so that each rider gets individual attention to correct her position in the saddle while the others are resting and more relaxed walking.

So we progress with teaching and correction. After a short time the whole ride is brought into the centre to rest and to ask questions. So that the ride can still remain on the right rein and yet the Instructor can see the position of the rider's legs, the ride should cross the school at the quarter marker, F to K or H to M. The Instructor can then stand outside the ride to correct the position of the legs. It should be pointed out to the riders that, when riding cross saddle or lunging a horse, they should use the left rein to compensate for the right rein work done while the rider is learning her position on a side saddle. Some Instructors do work on the left rein even during the first lesson because they like to see the position of the rider on the left rein, but it will be found that most riders do tend to come out and away from their pommels when working to the left.

To have someone on the ground to watch and correct when the pupil starts riding side saddle is essential. It can be a friend who has watched some lessons, but better still a side saddle rider. Once the pupil has had a little experience and wishes to carry on, then it is time for her to start looking for a saddle (see Chapter 5, page 34) because it is better to be able to put in some practice between each lesson.

3
IMPROVING THE RIDER

A good rider should never be complacent; little faults creep in. Think of the great riders and their teachers or trainers – they aim for perfection – none of us are likely to attain it, but it gives a purpose to riding and an interest to both rider and horse. We all have little mannerisms, some are charming, giving a person individuality, but some just spoil the effect and position of the horse and hamper his ability to move effortlessly under the rider. This is where the eye on the ground is so important, someone who can keep a picture in their mind and help the rider in front of them. The rider must be elegant in a side saddle, elegance is the main charm of this kind of riding. With a stronger and more secure seat the rider should be able to give the impression of harmony between her horse and herself, and the aids should be very much a secret between them. No clumsy use of the rein or whip, but a demonstration of willingness to obey from the horse and sympathy from the rider. 'No secrets so close as the aids between the horse and rider'; I have always liked this quotation from *Mr Sponge's Sporting Tour* by R.S. Surtees and often quote it when teaching.

The better understanding we have with our horses the more satisfaction we shall get from our riding. So we must consider the ways in which we communicate with the horse, that is the way we use our body weight, hands and legs, plus the stick which is the replacement of our right leg. The side saddle rider is deprived of the use of one leg, so in my opinion the other leg should only be carefully used, since it must be comparable to her stick to keep her horse straight, so the rider should use her back and weight to balance and control her horse as much as possible. The lightest pressure of the leg is answered once the horse realises that it is not always being pushed by the leg; with a good position of the knee on the saddle the leg is free to give the three delicate aids – calf, lower leg and heel or spur. At the beginning it was explained to the new side saddle rider that the position in the saddle has nothing to do with the leg on the horse and the knee off the saddle. It is an old-fashioned position of the leg, the aids are delicate. The calf means 'please', the lower leg says 'really you must' and the heel/spur 'come on, do not disobey'. Disobedience can be corrected with the stick and the heel plus the voice. This aid is particularly effective and useful since it can praise, appease and correct; the horse when training can rely on the voice never to give the wrong command when the legs can often contradict. The aid of the voice is so often forgotten these days – it is in my opinion a very important aid, it was the first aid that the horse learnt in his life working on the lunge. It is to him the same as our ABC is to us.

Usually most horses go so well side saddle that except with a very idle, inattentive horse the stick is not used except to balance and support the horse on circles and turns. In the old days sensitive horses, particularly mares, seemed always to go well for us women out hunting and give their best, and this is still true today. However I do realise that during the winter months we were unlikely to have problems with mares coming into season.

The Rider's Hands
How do we get good hands and be one of those people we hear about who have beautiful hands and for whom every horse goes well? The hands must be sympathetic yet positive; the horse is so much stronger than we are, brute force cannot really control him, he has to be humoured and persuaded to do as we wish. Perhaps we could use the phrase 'Equestrian Tact' which used to be used very often in days gone by. It has always been an accepted fact that the side saddle rider's hands are better than her cross saddle counter-part, because of the independent seat she has owing to her position in the saddle. I use the word 'in' because she must sit down in the saddle and not perch on top, having a stiff back which in turn means a stiff body. The arms must be relaxed and moveable, the wrist slightly bent so that the thumbs are held on top, the little fingers pointing slightly towards the body.

In my young days people were simply said to be born either with or without good hands but today we analyse things much

IMPROVING THE RIDER

more. There are three mains joints in the arm which affect the rider's hands: the wrist, the elbow and the shoulder. The hand itself has two very important functions connected with the reins: the wrist which should work as the hinge of a door, and the fingers which should move giving gentle communication to the horse's mouth and keeping up what was once known as 'conversation with the horse', but not an irritating jerking of the reins. It will be found that with a relaxed elbow and wrist the weight of the hand will open the elbow. Hold the hand up and allow it to fall. The elbow works as if it is attached to the arm on elastic, thus having a giving action to the forward movement of the horse, yet it can resist the horse's forward movement by merely ceasing to follow that movement. The shoulder should also be relaxed to allow the arm to function. Perhaps one might consider the three joints in reverse order, as they are all equally dependent on each other. A good position enables the rider to use her hands correctly.

The back must not be forgotten, a straight back with a neck which is the continuation of the spine supports the head on top of the spine – thus the rider sits up allowing the body to function correctly, following and absorbing the movement of the horse under her. So often we see either stiffness or over-suppleness which becomes sloppiness in the saddle and too much movement in the saddle. A comfortable horse with smooth paces helps the side saddle rider to look elegant and remain poised, yet effective, in the saddle.

The *Reins* themselves are important to the rider. Some of us prefer narrow reins because we have small hands, while others, especially the younger generation, prefer wider reins. I feel that a certain amount of delicate touch is lost with clumsy reins, but comfort to the hands is of major importance. A longer rein than the usual cross saddle rein is needed for most side saddle riders. The common faults of today are the reins being held both too far forwards and too low down. Lightness can only come from relaxed and pliable hands, held more in the rider's lap which is the natural position of the hands. A lower, wider position is sometimes needed to make a horse come down onto the bit and flex, but in the old days we would have changed the bit to get the horse to accept or have respect for the bit. When using a higher port or longer cheek piece to the curb, care must be taken to lighten the hand and keep a check on the position of the horse's head.

We all know that the side saddle rider has a stronger and more secure seat than her sister cross saddle, but if the horse really pulls, to resist the horse, especially with a horse who bears down, the hands can be fixed, the left behind the top pommel and the right hand behind the off-side saddle flap. This also puts the bit slightly at an angle in the horse's mouth so that he will find it more difficult to bear down in the rider's hands.

When showing or being photographed the rider should lengthen and lower her right hand to give more length of rein to her horse and more elegance to herself. Never be photographed on the near side – your skirt does not look as good as the view of your horse – with you sitting upright on him. Should your horse be difficult in the show ring, take a firm hold of the inside rein, flex his head to the right in England, but left in the USA and do not be afraid to control by use of the indirect rein; the horse will look better with a flexed head and he will not be able to play the fool with a firm controlling rein to the inside.

When using double reins it used to be the fashion to use plain reins, one thin and one thick, but I have found it better to have reins which are easily distinguished by their feel in the fingers. Therefore one plaited or laced rein with the curb rein plain can give a nice feel in the hands. Should you wish to use a rubber covered rein out hunting, it should be dark brown, not red or white, so that it looks as much like leather as possible.

I believe in saving the double bridle for special occasions such as hunting, competitions, or just a special hack out when you want to have real pleasure with a horse light in the hand. It is rather the same as wearing your best clothes every day – they become very ordinary, rather used and not so smart – so the same can happen with a double bridle on a horse. I feel when I put my double bridle on my horse, he should say to himself, 'Something special, fun perhaps', and be on his toes. Of course it is possible to ride in a double bridle and never use the curb rein, and the rider should practise with four reins in the hands so that they become easy to the fingers; I am merely saying do not use the best bridle too often or the horse will lose respect for it. In the old days snaffles were for exercise and schooling, doubles were for pleasure – you and your horse felt proud. One never asked for more collected paces in side saddle except in a double bridle. We did not expect our horses to flex and carry themselves in a snaffle.

Here I should mention a double bridle to me is a bridle with four reins and a curb chain, in other words I have found that some horses go better in the Pelham bridle, the curb rein to be used for collection and a better way of going. This bit, although despised by the purists can be very useful. I would always use the bit the horse prefers. You may find that a horse with a difficult mouth may go well for some time in a Pelham and after a time will accept the more conventional bridoon and curb bit. Remember, comfort in the mouth and acceptance of the bit or bits is important to the overall picture of rider and horse – in fact I used to use a jointed Pelham on one show pony who had a broken jaw – in this type of bit the curb chain does not come into use, it is there merely for appearance's sake and I have got away with this type of bit on young horses in the ring as well. Except when riding in a dressage competition, a Pelham can be used. Some horses prefer a single bit in their mouths to more of a mouthful and a Pelham can be used with roundings and a single rein for novices and children. It will be found that it gives more control and confidence to the rider and one usually gets better paces from the horse.

The reins are our closest communication with the horse. Ever since I can remember I have heard it said that the greatest asset a side saddle rider has is that her hands are so much better than those of a cross saddle rider of the same calibre. This is because her seat is more secure, thus making her hands more easily independent of any movement of her body. One sees so many bad positions of the hands; recently at one of our biggest shows there were fourteen ladies in the ring and seven of them, in my opinion, had incorrect positions of the hands. One rider did have difficulty with her horse, but the rest in both Preliminary Judging and in the main ring were having more difficulty than necessary. Was it that they did not know or that they had never been told?

The hands in cross saddle or side saddle should be gentle yet positive. There should be a light contact, but the hands should be as still as possible yet following the movement of the horse.

Any movement should be intended as communication to the horse, not involuntary movements caused by tension of the arms carried from the rider's body movements. Think about the three main joints of the arm and remember they should be relaxed. The English talk a lot about the wrist and fingers, while Vienna talks about the elasticity of the elbow and the French stress the relaxed shoulder, straight back and the neck being an extension of the back bone upon which the head sits. The hands should be held with the thumbs uppermost, the fingers lightly closed on the reins and the thumbs holding the reins onto the first fingers. The rider can look down into her hands just to check that she can see her fingers, all of them, with the little finger nearest to the body. We are told in the *Young Lady's Equestrian Manual* that the hands should be three inches from her body; this does not leave much room for movement and the hands might get into a fixed position and lose the grace and movement of a sympathetic hand, so I would say 'comfortable and a little further than three inches'.

The Rising Trot
The question of the rising trot is often discussed, so I am including my thoughts on this subject. Modern side saddle riding is not connected as much with hunting as it was in my young days. Since there was no transport until the late 1920s and early 1930s and the vans then used were very unreliable, ladies often hacked to the meets and home again after hunting. It was said that to rise at the trot rested both horse and rider, so it was a very common sight to see ladies rising at the trot, out hacking, going to the meet or riding home after hunting. But it was also said that most side saddles gave horses sore backs, and few people would offer a horse to a lady to hunt side saddle. I do feel that the rising trot often causes the saddle to swing and thus rub the horse on the off-side of his wither.

   The fashion of using the rising trot on a side saddle has more or less died out, and it is not encouraged by the British Side Saddle Association. This brings me to a funny story – some years ago a certain dressage test asked for rising trot so I was asked to teach the children on my course to do it. There are two theories of how to do a rising trot, *a)* the rider rises from the knee giving a small lift of her seat upwards and forwards, i.e.,

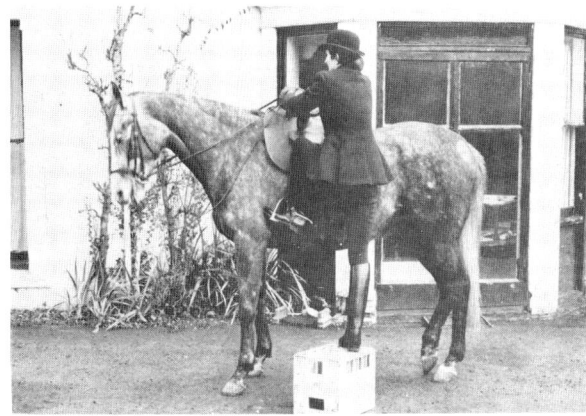

PLATE 1

(*left*) Mounting: (a) from mounting block, left hand with reins on the top pommel.

(*right*) Mounting: (b) sitting sideways, before putting right leg over top pommel.

(*left*) Mounting: (c) rider in the correct position.

PLATE 2

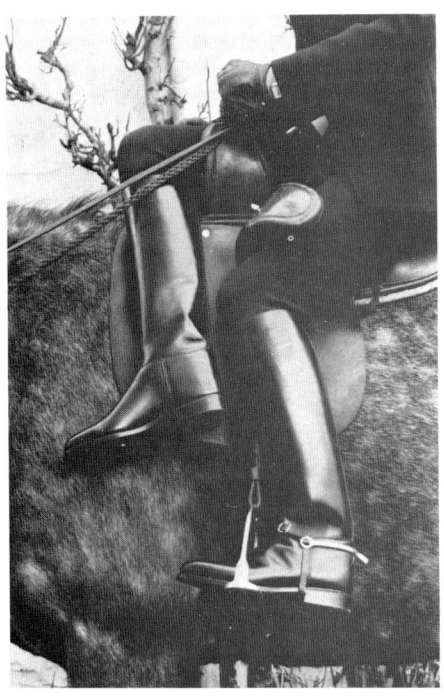

(*left*) Correct position of the legs.

(*below*) Good position of the hands.

PLATE 3

(*left*) Mrs Barham, one of the earliest supporters of the Side Saddle Association and now its Vice-President. Note the correctly tied stock and well-fitted veil.

(*below*) Correct dress for a Hack Class at small shows and before twelve o'clock at big shows.

PLATE 4

(*left*) Mayhew saddle.

(*right*) Owen saddle.

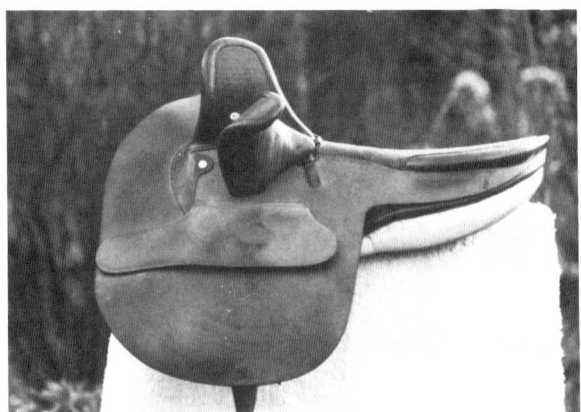

(*left*) Champion & Wilton saddle.

just rising out of the saddle and *b)* rising from the stirrup, which makes it easier to get a definite lift from the saddle but also makes it very easy in rising to swing out to the left, which I can remember so well seeing in the hunting field as a child when riding behind the field and hearing old Bill, our groom, say 'Look, there goes another sore wither on the off-side'. So I personally never teach rising trot from the stirrup. Anyway, the dressage test was duly ridden and afterwards the judge told me that she did not know if the children were really rising or just bumping in the saddle, since when I have never bothered to teach the rising trot. I consider it ineffective, bad for the horses' backs and apart from anything else it looks inelegant.

I was always made to sit hacking to a meet or coming home after hunting, since my father said, 'Do not rise going to a meet as your horse is to have a long day hunting and does not want his saddle moved', and coming home I was told, 'Sit still, your horse is tired enough without you trying to rise going home', so I never got into the habit of rising to the trot.

However the question of the rising trot must be left to the individual and any new conditions which are demanded from time to time. Recently at a Side Saddle Instructor's examination the rising trot was demonstrated as a method of showing the rider how to lift her weight forwards in preparation for the jumping position.

Lunging for the side saddle rider

After having learnt to lunge in 1947 I saw a great improvement in the way 'of going' in both my show ponies, Chocolate Box and Picture Play (we had won several Championships before Count Robert Orssich taught me to lunge in what I think of as the Continental Way). In those days few people lunged in England, instead they mostly long reined. The idea struck me one day, why not lunge with the rider on top of the horse, which I did and soon had great success with my daughter and her friends and there was a marked improvement in their riding. Since then I have used the lunge a great deal to help me as an Instructor.

I have found lunging the side saddle rider invaluable: one can position a rider by asking her to place the right hand on the balance strap and the left hand on the top pommel. The placing of the hands hold the rider's body in the correct position, the rider feels secure and it is safe to let the horse move under her. Anyone can walk, trot or canter, in five minutes, should you be letting an audience 'have a go' on a side saddle at a Riding Club Side Saddle evening. Having got the feeling of the horse moving, the rider will know in ten minutes whether she likes the feeling or hates it. The majority are interested and feel there may be something in looking further into side saddle riding. After all it is something different and, taught correctly, much more secure for a round legged rider, who finds her legs wobble on a cross saddle. If one is to teach on the lunge either astride or side saddle, it is very important to have a really well-schooled reliable horse to work with, one that you can trust, and that you have ridden on the lunge yourself so you know exactly what it feels like. For side saddle a very smooth trot and canter help so much. I do not mind if the horse does a four time canter, it makes the canter easier to sit to for the beginner. The person with the lunge rein can easily push the horse on into a correct three time canter when she wishes to. On the flat, side reins are useful because they control the gaits and pace better and give the rider a feel of the horse's movement. With a horse one can trust, the Instructor can concentrate on the teaching and techniques to be passed on to the rider. It is easy for the rider to concentrate on her position in the saddle when the horse is controlled by the lunge rein and whip. She can get the feel of where and how to sit and alter her position as her Instructor mentions corrections. The exercises are far better executed on the lunge when the hands are free from the reins. All the exercises (see pages 14–16) are aimed at correcting faults seen in the rider. The rider can get the 'feel' which is so important to the side saddle rider because her seat and her back are her main aids. She can learn to push her horse forward and use her weight to slow her horse down. This is a wonderful way of demonstrating to the rider that her reins are not as important as most people feel them to be.

If the Instructor can have someone competent to lunge for her it is invaluable, since the position of the legs is so important and the rider can then be seen from both sides. Likewise with beginners always work on the right rein first so that the rider's weight is directed automatically into her pommels and not out of them. Some may say that to do this will make the horse uneven by working mostly to the right, but if the horse is worked mostly on the left with a cross saddle rider this will compensate. When the beginner improves then she can be taught in a confined area such as a covered school to use her left leg, as since she has learned to use her left knee to keep herself up on top of her saddle she will not be in the same danger of falling to the left as she would have done as a complete beginner. Lunging to the left can commence when she has begun to establish her position in the saddle.

Even an advanced rider and her horse can benefit from a correct lunge lesson. It improves them both and gives better co-ordination between horse and rider. Every rider can benefit by working through the exercises and getting a better feel in her seat. It gives the rider time to concentrate on her position in the saddle without having to control her horse, so that she can alter any part of her body as directed and get the feel of what is correct, learning to absorb the movement of her horse under her.

When starting to learn to jump she can get the feeling of putting the weight onto the forward part of her right thigh and balancing with the movement of the horse. The rider's seat should be slightly raised out of the saddle, she can balance better if she places her hands forward on a neck strap or the horse's mane. First do this on the flat at the walk because it is smoother, then at the trot before introducing trotting poles on the ground. If this exercise can be done on the circle the Instructor can watch the position of the legs, and from the outside of the circle when someone is holding the lunge for her. For teaching jumping, one should not use a horse which either stops or rushes its fences. The horse for this work must have a calm approach, yet be forward going so that the rider can have confidence and concentrate on her position.

Teaching jumping
The position of ladies in the side saddle has followed that of men where jumping is concerned. Pictures prior to 1914 show all ladies and gentlemen leaning well back when taking fences out hunting, but by the late 1930s Mrs Houblon is leaning well forwards. The position of the rider changed from backwards to

forwards. During the changeover Mrs Marshall showed a midway seat and show-jumped sitting in the middle of her saddle but not interfering with her horse – see *To Whom the Goddess* by Lady Apsley and Lady Diana Shedden – but that was before the Italian forward seat was really accepted. In 1932 Santini, who pioneered the forward seat, wrote about side saddle jumping after which all riders tried to follow the movement of the horse.

The side saddle rider should start by getting a *forward position* in her saddle, balancing on her right knee and easing her weight out of the saddle. To do this it is best to work on the lunge. The main difficulty will be found in keeping the right shoulder back, for this is by far the most common fault with all side saddle riders whether they are jumping or riding on the flat. However this can easily be corrected by asking the rider to put her left hand forward onto the horse's mane or neck strap and her right hand back on the balance strap; this keeps the rider's body straight and allows her weight to be carried forward in the saddle (see exercise three on page 15). Some riders feel more confident with a slightly shorter stirrup, which brings the left leg nearer the leaping head, but one should still be able to slip one's hand between the leaping head and the lower thigh, too tight a left leg into the leaping head brings stiffness, and the rider often jerks on landing.

Start jumping by walking and trotting over poles on the ground, sitting back and taking the ordinary position after completing the exercise and returning again to the forward position when next approaching the poles. When the rider feels confident with this exercise, then move the poles to canter spacing, but be careful not to overdo it at first, nor to make the rider ache. Each day try to progress, from the trotting poles to cavaletti and then on to small cross poles, followed by a course of jumps of not more than 45 cms (1ft 6ins) in height. When practising at home, there is no harm in the rider holding on to her horse's mane and balance strap to help her to consolidate her position over any size of fence. Some riders prefer a rubber tread in their stirrups; this is not easy with an ordinary side saddle iron, as most have three bars on the tread, so it means taking an ordinary cross saddle iron and having the stirrup leather's stitches cut and restitched on. You can find some side saddle irons with rubber treads – I had one in 1936.

It must be remembered with a pupil riding cross saddle or side saddle that some riders do find it very difficult to relax and swing with their horses, but as I have already said confidence is the key to the rider relaxing. When considering relaxing, it is well to think about the 'emergency grip', talked about in many books, when the rider is advised to raise the right toe and grip with the left knee. This results in the rider tensing the right leg muscles. I find it much better in fact to keep the right toe down, for this helps the right thigh to rest on the saddle and support you more than tight muscles which will push the rider off the safe of the saddle, but each rider must suit herself. When hunting a lot in the 1920s and 1930s I did get a lump (probably quite incorrectly) on my left thigh where it met the leaping head, but in those days no-one ever discussed riding methods or positions – some rode badly, some were natural horsemen/women – for it was considered bad form to discuss how people rode their horses.

This forward position is only correct for jumping over fences without a drop, but when jumping over unknown country out hunting it is wise to watch someone jump in front of you so as to be prepared for drop fences, when a more central position would be wiser than a forward seat position.

Once you have built up your pupil's confidence you will find that her jumping becomes much more relaxed.

4
CLOTHES AND TRADITION

Clothes and tradition are so closely bound together and the saying, 'My dear it is just **not** done' must be borne in mind. In the 1920s, when I first became aware of what one should or should not wear, we were governed by our elders. Side saddle clothes were very formal; it was considered very bad taste to draw attention to oneself by wearing loud colours, just as a man should not wear a hacking jacket with loud checks. In summer we hardly rode, since the horses were turned out to grass. The hounds were exercised by walking them around the fields, or by taking them around the roads, the grooms riding bicycles or later riding the cub hunting cobs when proper exercise started before the cubbing season. For hound exercise or hacking we wore our oldest habit apron and a buff 'Holland' jacket made of the same unbleached linen as our kennel coats. No-one dreamt of riding without an apron.

The modern coat of the habit should have two vents in the back, the skirt of the habit, always referred to as an 'apron', should be long enough to cover the rider's right foot when mounted and should hang in a straight line along the hem, which should be suitably weighted to remain in position when galloping or jumping.

For showing, women wore the same clothes as for hunting except for the coats which were of a lightweight material, the apron still being of double weight material so that it hung well. For hunting a double weight coat was usually worn, with a double lining of serge and silk. In those days our coats were long and rested on the horses' backs, therefore they had a waterproof lining on the tails so that the horses' sweat could be easily washed off after hunting. Breeches were made of the same material, they fitted tightly, the buttons on the right leg being on the inside, and had detachable wash leather linings which were tacked into the seat to enable them to be removed

CLOTHES AND TRADITION

and washed. Later when ladies started to ride astride winged breeches became fashionable so that a lady could ride astride or side saddle. Having shown horses myself in both hunter and hack classes I knew that often there would not be time for me to go back to my horse box and change my breeches between classes, so I saw to it that a rule allowing light breeches to be worn under a side saddle habit was included in our British rules. While in the USA recently I saw the rule of dark breeches only, causing problems for one rider at a Show. Of course it does look nice to have dark breeches, but if the habit fits well and the rider sits correctly, one should not notice the light breeches.

Hunting boots usually had patent leather legs and calf leather feet – they were shorter than those worn today, reaching just to mid-calf, so they were loose and comfortable. Our aprons covered them, as in those days we did not even show our boots, the aprons being 2-4 inches below the boots. Only when ladies started to ride cross saddle did boots become as today, longer and tighter, to show off the leg in the boot. We never wore garters. Even today in my mind to wear a garter on the right leg is unecessary, for if the buckle slips it can scratch the saddle and could be uncomfortable, and since we do not wear buttons on our breeches any longer where should the lady put the garter strap, which used traditionally to lie between the top and second button? How this wearing of garters came about I have no idea, it suddenly appeared. It is impossible for a judge to check the right garter without disarranging the rider's apron. It does not appear to be mentioned in either our British rules or those of the International Side Saddle Association of America.

Clothes are always a personal taste, but side saddle clothes are practical and the items listed by the Side Saddle Association were discussed in Committee before the following was agreed as correct turn out:

Rider Side saddle habit of restrained hue, long boots (black or brown), gloves (not black), no buttonholes, no jewellery. SSA badges may be worn.

Juniors: At all levels should wear a hunting cap or safety hat without a veil, with a collar and tie. They may wear a blunt spur, but it is not compulsory, and a cane or whip no longer that 76 cms (30 ins). The hair should be exceptionally neat and tidy.

Hair ribbons should be black, brown or navy.

Adults: At all levels should wear a safety bowler but with a veil, collar and tie and the hair should be worn in a bun, artificial or otherwise. Top hats with a veil may be worn at the National Show and in any qualifying class which takes place in the afternoon. Where any show holds a qualifying class divided into Preliminary and Final judging, a top hat should only be worn for the Final judging. When wearing a top hat a hunting tie (stock) is compulsory. Adults will wear a blunt spur or spur band and carry a whip or cane not more than 1 metre in length.

Horse. Side saddle and conventional bridle with bit. Bridles with double reins (double or Pelham) should be worn if the rider is wearing a top hat.

NB: Long Boots (black or brown). It should be noted that brown boots are only worn with a brown or tweed habit, known as 'ratcatcher', then a brown bowler hat is allowed, otherwise all bowlers should be black.

It is recommended that the shirt worn should be white, light blue, or pin-striped with a neat fitting high collar (a boy's shirt is ideal), worn with a tie. A polka dot tie is always smart or club type of tie, tied in a small neat knot. A large floppy collar gives a blowzy effect. A waistcoat is traditional – yellow, beige or Tattershall check look smart, red is inadvisable as it draws attention to the chest and rather hits the eye.

I admit that I had a large hand in the discussions as I had seen the rather theatrical approach which some riders produced with their own ideas on dress. Stress was laid on the feminine side in the aim of the revival of side saddle, 'this elegant form of riding'. So my 'hunting eyes' were startled and amazed to see some colours presented I had never thought of, and quite unsuitable materials. One lady said proudly, 'I made it myself for my daughter'. How could I tell her that the material was so thin it showed the pommels of the saddle in an ugly line, the pommels did not fit her daughter's legs and the colour was just not acceptable except in a musical ride for colour interest! Velvet collars were produced. Aprons blew in the wind and looked more like large curtains draped over the rider's legs than side saddle skirts. Of course this was all frowned upon by the diehards of the hunting world and caused a lot of criticism from certain judges of side saddle hacks and hunters.

In fact a meeting was called at Wembley to discuss the new Ladies' Side Saddle Association. Having joined the Association I felt it was better to try and help than condemn and said so, but there seemed to be a grave lack of understanding of how to wear the clothes which were second nature to us hunting women and there became a rift between us and the new side saddle riders. For example, top hats of queer shapes were worn on the back of the head and a plum coloured habit and matching top hat appeared on a child in the show ring. All this was frowned upon, hence the dictation of what was acceptable, after we had formed an Advisory Committee.

A veil is a must for both bowler and top hat, a neat tight fitting one looks best. I like silk veils as they are more comfortable to wear and fit the face better; the cotton net is harsh and should the veil be too large takes on a beekeeper's look. The veil should be pinned around the bun to secure the hat. Even if the bun is a false one it should never be attached to the hat elastic because it can come off and losing a hat is most infra-dig and embarrassing – as I saw recently in the show ring. Even if you need to wear a false bun, (I have worn one for some years now as I have short hair), there is no need for it to be insecure. Place a hair net over your own hair, pin the false bun into your own hair and the net, then cover all with another hair net (the fine nylon type with elastic, not the clumsy slumber type net). Last of all pin your veil over the bun – nothing will then move your hat or your bun.

When wearing a top hat, wear a folded stock in the show ring, and for hunting a properly tied stock (hunting tie). The pin I am told should be placed across the tie. I think as children, we, my brother and I, used pins in under the chin downwards – probably we were wrong. Silk stocks are more comfortable and do look very elegant if properly tied but they are more difficult to tie correctly than white piqué, which looks whiter and I think just a little smarter.

5
SADDLERY

The history of the development of the side saddle is a very interesting subject and a whole book such as *The Saddle of Queens* can be devoted to it. Here I will merely touch very lightly on it saying that, in 1560 Queen Elizabeth I rode completely sideways on official occasions such as inspecting her troops, but out hunting we see from a woodcut that she used a saddle with one central horn or pommel. Catherine de Medici introduced a saddle with two horns or pommels through which the right thigh passed. In 1835 the leaping head was introduced in France and by 1850 was used extensively and ladies were able to gallop and jump on almost equal terms with gentlemen. Since then the second pommel became reduced in size to a mere hump on the off-side of the saddle. These saddles can be very comfortable as the flat top encourages the rider's weight onto the right thigh.

Originally ladies' side saddles with one or two pommels used to have a variety of genteel foot rests, where the toes or whole foot was placed on a small stirrup on which the left foot rested. The most usual were versions of the Devon Slipper, later followed by a rest for the toes and ball of the foot known in my day as a 'clog'. But after 1835 and the introduction of the leaping head women really no longer just 'graced the meets' but followed hounds as well. There was a vogue of using men's stirrup irons and since all the saddles in use then had roller bars or plain dees the stirrup did not fall from the saddle if there was an accident and often women were dragged and this usually resulted in severe head injuries. As a result of this after 1860 different sorts of safety stirrup irons were invented and as with so many things to do with side saddles there were three main types. These were the Scott, the Cope and the Latchford. The Scott and the Cope worked by a release mechanism; the inner stirrup of the Scott opened at the top when the foot came out of position and the toe came up to the centre of the small stirrup, the Cope worked by opening at the bottom. With both these types one must be careful not to put the stirrup on back to front; the flat bar has to face towards the rider's heel while the rounded bar faces forwards. The Latchford worked on the principle of having a detachable stirrup inside a larger one, and there are many other variations on these patterns by other manufacturers. Indeed, only recently when we were taking photographs for this book I found three others on the Copes patent, the York, the Wheeler and the Bradbury.

In the 1920s my father always insisted that we not only used safety irons but also safety catches which would release the leather as well as the iron. Mine was a Champion & Wilton, whilst my aunt's was an Owen which I still have today. This belt and braces approach made doubly sure that if we did fall then we were very unlikely to be dragged since it was an extremely remote possibility that both safety devices would fail to work. Nowadays no-one seems to use safety irons, but if you have an old side saddle with a roller bar it is essential that you use a safety stirrup and not an ordinary stirrup iron. Finding a safety iron can be a problem for, as with so many things these days, many have gone abroad having been bought for their ornamental and curiosity value by foreign collectors. In this country safety stirrups can be found decorating public house walls, and safety stirrups fetch fairly fancy prices with the prices getting fancier with the more rust the iron has! However, it is possible to buy new safety stirrups as they are now made in France.

Later the main changes to side saddles were the size of the pommel and plain leather seats that replaced the more ornamental quilted ones of the 1890s. In their turn suede and doeskin seats have replaced the more practical leather seats. By 1910 safety stirrup bars had replaced the roller bar stirrup fitting. Since then the pommels have become wider and less curved. In the early 1930s Mrs Archer Houblon with Miss Mayhew developed the Improved Leaping Head, to make it easier for the side saddle rider to get forward in her saddle when jumping and following the principle of the Italian forward seat. Since then the modern side saddle rider has felt that the saddles made in the 1930 to 1945 period were the best. Recently through experimenting with modern materials, Mr Swain of Walsall has been making new saddles with more comfortable pommels and suede seats which are softer than the pre-war saddles. These saddles are made on copies of the Owen type tree. The Side Saddle Association in conjunction with Miss Dod Noble and Mrs Robertson of Sandon Saddlery helped Messrs Olton and Butler to produce a new side saddle tree of laminated wood with metal fittings. It is on these trees and old trees that all new side saddles are made today.

Side saddles were made by nearly every local saddler in the early twentieth century, using the attachments for stirrups of the three main famous firms in London who made ladies' side saddles, so that unless the saddle is stamped with the firm's name on the pommel or saddle flaps they were not necessarily made by Champion & Wilton, Mayhew or Owen.

To help the hunting woman and enable a wet saddle to dry more quickly Robson of York made a saddle with ventilation holes in the leather covering the panels. With the same aim in mind the Wykeham Pad was introduced and used by Champion & Wilton, Mayhew and Owen. This was a felt lining to any saddle, the idea being that the thick felt was shaped to fit a particular horse, so that a lady with four horses had one saddle with four different shaped pads, which could be washed and dried, thus overcoming the problem of drying wet hunting saddles for the next day. Unfortunately the thick felt used for these pads seems to be almost unobtainable these days. However new panels can be fitted to these skeleton saddles.

Later Champion & Wilton bought up both the Mayhew and Owen companies, and they adopted the skirt of the Mayhew saddles as being more practical and neat, and they also changed their own balance strap fitting, as it was not so practical as the plain strap used by both the other firms. In the early part of the twentieth century there was in New York and, we are told, in London, a firm called Martin & Martin. They followed the fashion in ladies' saddles but also invented the well-known Martin & Martin spring on and off side flap; this is easily used and keeps the saddle flap down without the necessity of using a surcingle. They, and other firms from England, used the idea of controlling the length of stirrup by a strap connected with the balance girth. This proved impractical as when the horse needed its girth tightening so the stirrup leather became too long; as a result this type of fitting was not used for long. The modern side saddle leather is altered by a hook fastening which is covered by a leather sleeve, smooth side towards the lady's boot.

In England the new side saddle rider, when looking for a saddle can use her Side Saddle Association local Chairman or instructor for advice about how and where to look for a side saddle. The first thing to do is to find a saddle which is comfortable for her to sit in so that her left thigh can easily fit under the leaping head. It will be found that saddles with narrow pommels fit more shapes of thighs than the wider and more fashionable pommels, and that leather-seated saddles are quite comfortable and not as slippery as they are made out to be. It is possible to buy a sheepskin 'seat saver' to fit any saddle, these are comfortable and very usable, perhaps not in Equitation classes, although one would only lose one mark on 'turn out'. So think on the lines of a cheaper saddle to start and work up, unless you can afford the best from the start.

The saddle must fit the rider: one can always ride in a saddle slightly too big for one, but not in one too small. Most saddles can have their stuffing altered to fit your horse but a general or medium fitting saddle is the most likely to fit more horses than a narrow or wide tree. So first look for a good make of saddle, train your eye by looking at many saddles, get your experienced friends to help you, for they will have more knowledge of what to look for and remember the three great names: Mayhew, Owen and Champion & Wilton. Robson of York who used Mayhew stirrup attachments is also good. Martin & Martin saddles are not often found in England but they are comfortable. If in difficulties get in touch with the Secretary of the Side Saddle Association; she knows where there are secondhand saddles for sale through the Side Saddle Association's secondhand agency.

Should the saddle you have found and like have no stirrup this is no problem, for the attachments of all three makes of saddle can be obtained from Mr Barry Swain of 53 Main Street, Stonnall, Nr Walsall, Staffordshire, England. The Owen is the most expensive, the Mayhew next and the Champion & Wilton is the cheapest.

No really good secondhand saddles costs less than £450, and new ones cost around £550 – that is in England in 1987. For some unknown reason some riders are even willing to pay more for nice older saddles. It will be found that each saddle usually needs fitting to the individual horse, but there are those rare saddles that seem to fit every horse and most riders.

One of the most important parts of the saddle are the girths and balance strap. Since the side saddle has to be more tightly adjusted than a cross saddle in which the rider is more centrally positioned, having one leg each side of the horse, wider girths are used to spread the load. Most saddles have three straps, those with two girth straps were usually meant for showing rather than hunting. Depending on the fit of the saddle it is usual to use the first two straps or the first and third straps because we tend not to use the three buckled girths these days. It is a wise precaution to have a woollen or serge liner folded into the centre of the girth; this is kept oiled so that the girth remains supple and soft because leather girths can become very hard and cause girth galls. The girths should be wide so that the balance strap will not slip off the girth and cause pinching of the flesh between it and the girth, and for this reason avoid using a Balding girth. The Fitzwilliam girth, very much favoured for hunting in the 1920s, was a wide cotton or woollen girth with a narrower girth slotted through two keepers at the top and bottom of the wider girth, and these three buckles were attached to the three girth straps. An ordinary two buckled cross saddle girth of lampwick which is soft and easily kept clean is good.

The modern balance strap or girth is a neat strap of approximately 3 cm (1½ins) with a plain buckle at one end and a buckle with two or three keepers into which the end of the balance girth is neatly tucked. A half balance strap can be used; it is favoured for showing as it looks neat, but I do not recommend it for use by beginners who need their saddle held firmly in place for them, nor do I favour it for hunting although I do know that many ladies use them.

The shape of the modern side saddle stirrup iron is not as elegant or neat as the lady's iron of fifty years ago, in fact some side saddle irons are clumsy in appearance. I do realise that ladies' boots have altered in shape and are more practical and not so light as Mrs Hayes advised in books from 1893 to 1920, also I think ladies' feet have become larger since it is no longer the fashion to have small feet and we are on our feet more than my generation was, gone are the days when we sat and sewed until tea time! Most ladies' irons have three bars on the treads,

SADDLERY

so it is difficult to fit a rubber tread; should you wish to do so then use a cross saddle iron adapted as mentioned on page 28. Nowadays we never see the type of iron I used to use with an inset rubber tread in a solid iron. These were heavy, hung well and were easy to slip one's foot into.

Sticks As the lady's right leg is replaced by her stick it must be solid, not clumsy but hard enough to press on a horse's side to replace the right leg aid. At first a horse which is new to side saddle work may need more help than when he knows how to work in a side saddle, when it will be found that the stick is hardly used. When schooling a lazy horse the rider might need a long schooling whip, but dressage whips bend too much to be of any real use to the side saddle rider. A hunting crop should be carried when hunting or in Ladies' Hunter classes in the show ring; these are carried mostly to keep hounds away from one's horse's heels but can be used as a reminder very effectively if the horse needs correction. For pleasure, hacking and showing, I always carry a moderately long leather-bound cane. The one metre (one yard) canes are heavy in the hand and look clumsy but in my opinion nothing looks more out of place than a long wobbling dressage whip stuck out miles from the horse's side or flapping on his side.

The *bridle* should suit the horse and look correct. It would be silly to ride a cob or a hunter in a light bridle with a rolled noseband and coloured brow band made for a hack. A thicker, more workmanlike bridle of bigger dimensions suits the longer intelligent head of a hunter, and the wider nose band makes his face look more attractive, whereas the narrower leather shows off the elegant head of a hack or riding horse. The snaffle bridle is much favoured today as a kind bridle, but because the lady's one leg lacks the ability to drive the horse forward into its bit it will be found a horse goes better in perhaps a Vulcanite Pelham or little double bridle. Sometimes a half moon curb bit is the answer. There is no need to use the curb rein all the time. It will be found that horses enjoy wearing a double bridle if it is correctly fitted and used. It makes the difference of a delicate light touch rather than a heavy contact to obtain the same answer from your horse.

Here a point about double bridles should perhaps be mentioned. So many of the modern curb bits are shaped with straight upper branches above the bit, whereas the old-fashioned ones broaden slightly outwards, thus following the shape of the horse's jaw line and so do not pinch. It is sometimes difficult to find a bit that fits both the mouth and the cheek of a horse; comfort in the mouth is essential and many horses fuss in a double bridle these days. I myself favour a fixed mouth piece for most horses. A horse with a slightly larger tongue will find a half moon bit with a slight port will give more tongue room. Horses with Arab blood in them have two problems – a thick jaw bone, making flexing less easy and a thick tongue making some straight bar bits uncomfortable. It will be found that the bridoon is seldom considered and only the same bit as always is used. There are some nice little bridoons with flat rings or French links, and sometimes one of the check bits will prove very useful on a horse that is a bit strong headed or bores. As long as the hands are light it is better to use a sharper bit gently rather than a thick bit and have to tug. A lady should not have to fight her horse. If the horse is correctly schooled with two legs he will very quickly go well with one leg supported by the rider's back and weight and her stick. Most horses do not need a lot of schooling with a side saddle on. Often in the old days my daughter and I were asked to ride a horse side saddle for someone at shows and afterwards would be told that the horse had never worn a side saddle before, and they usually had gone very well.

Saddling up   It is important that the side saddle rider learns how to put on her saddle because nowadays few people understand side saddles. The saddle should sit with two fingers breadth behind the shoulder blade. It should not sit on the shoulder itself because that would restrict the movement of the shoulder and prove uncomfortable for the rider, and it will be found that the saddle would then tend to sit higher in front, which would make the rider tip backwards and become behind the movement of the horse. The saddle should not be too long for it would then sit over the kidneys and be most uncomfortable for the horse.

A good side saddle should sit slightly to the right before the

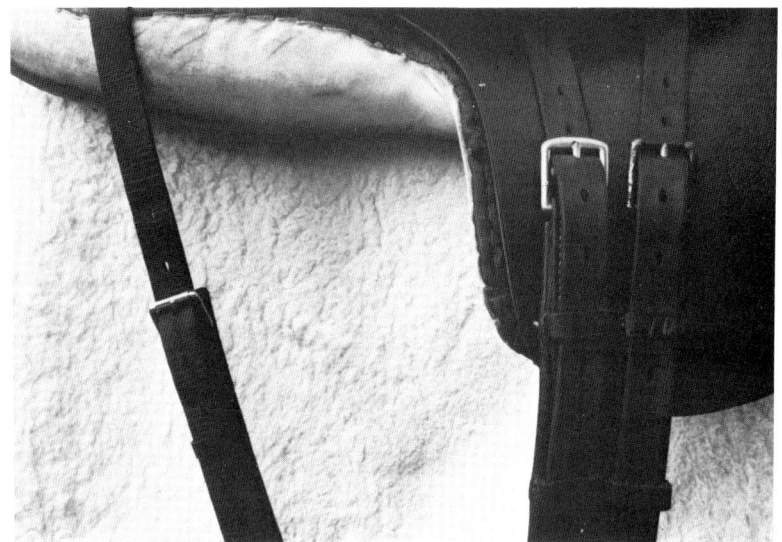

PLATE 5 (*above*) Offside of Mayhew saddle, showing outside girths together with three fold leather girth with keepers and full balance strap.

(*below, left*) Offside girth straps of Owen saddle. Compare these with the Champion & Wilton arrangement with a point strap and over girth strap (*right*).

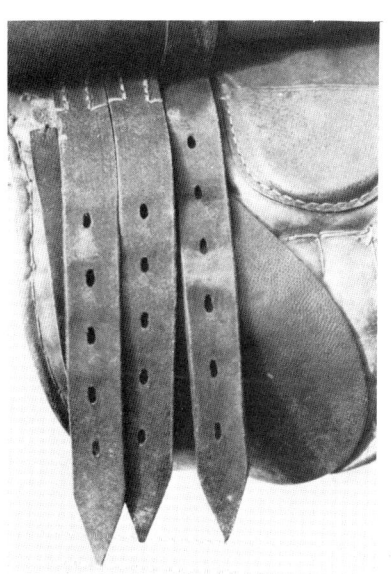

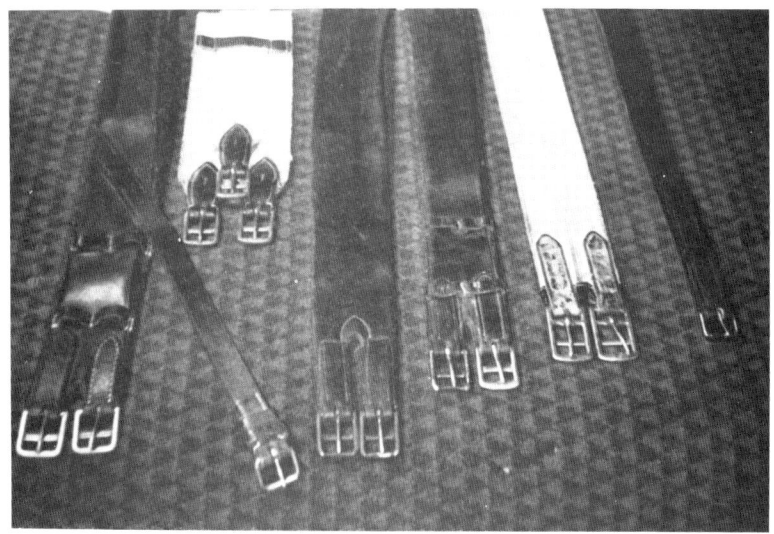

PLATE 6 (*above*) Girths: *from left to right* Three fold with half balance strap; Fitzwilliam; ordinary three fold; three fold with loops for outside girth straps; Lampwick; correct width full balance strap.

(*below*) Mayhew saddle, off side, showing balance strap (*left*) and Mayhew saddle, near side.

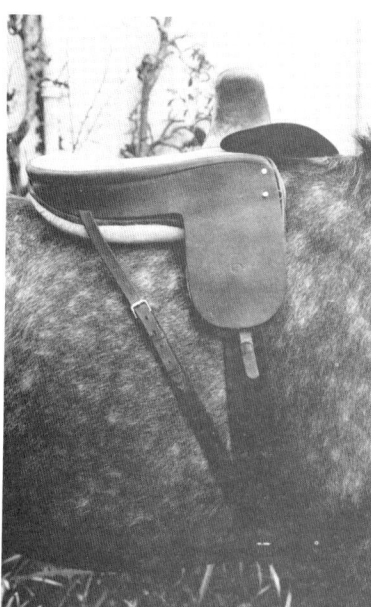

PLATE 7

(*right*) Mayhew safety stirrup bar.

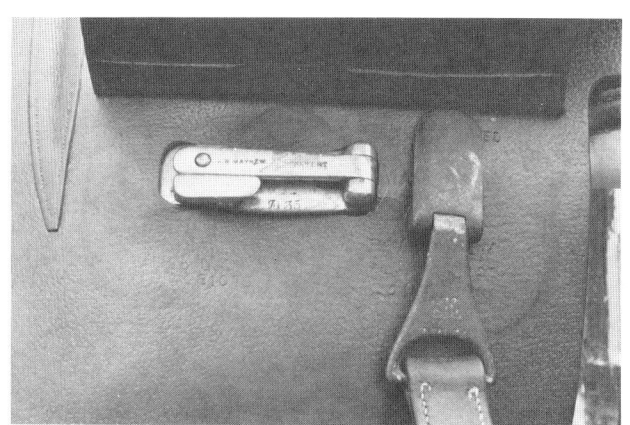

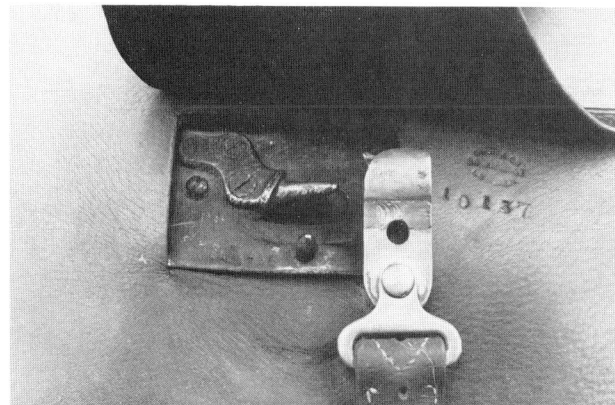

(*left*) Owen safety stirrup bar.

(*right*) Champion & Wilton safety stirrup bar.

PLATE 8 (*above*) Mrs Sims, the author's granddaughter, turning in mid air when jumping off against the clock to win at the Windsor Three Day event in 1986.

(*below*) Mrs Barham's first Display Team, Wembley, 1979.

rider mounts. This I was taught by Mr Wookey of Uttoxeter. I had asked him what was wrong, he looked at me pityingly and said most politely, 'Excuse me, madam, all good side-saddles should carry to the right until mounted.'

The stuffing of the panels should sit close to the horse's back, but beware that the bearing of the saddle does not pinch or press on the withers. Should the saddle not sit correctly try putting a numnah under the saddle and see if that improves the fit.

Unlike the cross saddle the girths are tightened on the off side. First buckle the girth, then the balance strap and lastly the flap strap. Remember to leave plenty of holes to tighten up the girth on the offside; tighten first on the near side before the rider mounts, so that she can adjust her girths on the off side.

The saddle may have exposed girth straps or the saddle may have a clip fastening on elastic which the rider can pull down and get at her girths or she may have a more old-fashioned saddle which has a fixed flap strap with a buckle more in the centre of the horse's stomach; some of these type of flap straps do have a keeper which will allow the flap to be slipped up to expose the girths and for these types of saddle the flap must be kept supple. In these days of no grooms it is wise to have these old-fashioned flap straps altered, for after a couple of hours out hunting or hacking or just before going into the ring at a show most horses need a pull at the girth.

6
CHOICE OF HORSE FOR SIDE SADDLE

Choosing any horse is a personal problem, and the suitability of a horse for the side saddle rider is the same: the horse's temperament and paces must suit the requirements of the individual. One cannot really choose a horse for someone else unless they like exactly the same type as you do yourself. The late Horace Smith (a well-known dealer and Riding Master) always said that a horse with a little knee action would always win a Side Saddle Show Class as it gave a better ride than a really extravagant mover. This old gentleman really knew the requirements of side saddle riders, since he had worked with London high society during the reigns of five Kings and Queens of England. His book *Riding Master* is well worth reading.

In the past ladies were told that they should never ride anything over 15.2 hh but it does depend on the lady who requires the horse. A small lady can ride a large horse better side saddle than cross saddle; I am only 5 feet and when I ride a 17.00 hh horse side saddle I feel less like a tom tit on a gatepost!

When looking at the horse's conformation there are three main factors to consider:

1. The shoulder and wither: a well defined shoulder will hold a side saddle in place better than round shoulders and an upright shoulder usually means that the horse will not have comfortable paces, but there are exceptions.

2. A good strong back, well ribbed up to take the weight of the rider who is sitting further back on her horse than when riding cross saddle. Sometimes a horse with a slightly long back will give a more comfortable ride side saddle.

3. Good quarters and a strong hind leg are assets since he has to carry the weight of his rider further back than a horse carrying a cross saddle, but again the rider will find out all this when she tries the horse. A sway back must be avoided since the saddle

CHOICE OF HORSE FOR SIDE SADDLE

will only rest on the shoulder and at the back of the saddle. Some cobs have a very bumpy trot which rules them out. The side saddle rider really needs a free forward-going horse, because she wants to feel she has her horse 'in her hands' as it is then ready to respond to her aids.

The novice's horse must be kind, obedient and very placid, whereas a lady who is going to enjoy herself needs a horse which, in my opinion, has a little gaiety about it, can have a little shy – a little laugh you might say – when they are out riding because you are not always going round in circles or perpetually riding in a covered school. Horses need to be out in the open and so do their riders. To get to know each other long rides in the country are great fun for the novice rider when she feels that she can ride for some time. Even if she gets tired, she can easily rest but it does mean that the horse and rider are enjoying themselves together. Companionship is a great thing between the horse and rider and this is developed more, I am sure, from riding in the country than by schooling in the field.

Each rider will have done a certain amount of work with an Instructor before they start riding properly and have found out what type of riding they want to do. So my advice to the beginner is to progress quietly, borrow a horse if you can, or hire a horse which is sensible and able to help you. When you have had six months on the hired horse perhaps you can change and ride something more lively and after this, if you are determined to get a horse of your own, seek the advice and help of your tutor or a member of the Side Saddle Association as to the suitability of a mount.

7
ADVICE TO INSTRUCTORS

Nothing and no-one is perfect in this imperfect world. But it is amazing how much we can help each other, and how co-operative our horses are, and how so few of them object to carrying a side saddle, when by all laws of the Medes and Persians they should do so. Should the horse not have carried a side saddle before it is wise to be cautious, but in all my long life I have only known two horses who were really difficult in this respect. Usually horses accept the saddle calmly and seem not to notice the difference in aids, and in five minutes all is well. It is probably best to lunge the horse at walk, trot and canter, then tighten up the balance strap and lead him in a small circle left and then right. With horses that are inclined to buck it might be prudent to use a half balance strap, but you should not use this kind of horse for teaching. In my opinion never use a half balance strap with beginners or novice riders who are bound to need a saddle securely held in place for them to start with – all beginners are inclined to let their weight slip slightly to the left off the top of the saddle, therefore they need the whole balance strap to hold the saddle securely.

The most important attribute, in my opinion, for any Instructor is to be able to put himself or herself into the place of the pupil in front of them. You may not find it a strange feeling to sit on a side saddle and you should not do so. But how many people in the past have jumped on the bandwagon and taught side saddle without ever having ridden it? It is easy to see what is wrong, but how best is that fault corrected? It is not easy to explain and put things right. I consider it best actually to show a beginner the correct position and explain why the rider should keep her weight on top of the right thigh to compensate for the weight of both legs on the left side – why you do not allow your right knee to press or lean into the top pommel – we are always told to have a hands breadth between the leaping head and the

ADVICE TO INSTRUCTORS

left leg – but I have never read that the right leg should have the feeling of rolling the weight onto the outside of the right thigh and that the hand should be able to pass just between the leg and the top pommel, except when the emergency grip is required in cases of bucking or some other similar problem. This position helps the rider to keep up on top of her saddle and helps her left knee to support her upward on top of the saddle. Open the left knee and show her how her weight immediately comes off her right thigh onto her left seat bone and left pendulous leg. Explain that side saddle riding has nothing to do with the dressage position of leg on the horse's side and knee off the saddle. It is perhaps best explained that the left leg is held in the old – almost military position – of the knee on the saddle, and the leg off the horse's side, so that the horse can feel the aids of the leg and answer them quickly. When the leg is held on the horse's side it pushes the knee off the saddle.

In my young days we were not really taught to ride – corrected occasionally by parents and grooms, yes, but not taught, no. Country children just rode as town children walked in the park, or had lessons from a riding master. We caught horses and ponies from the fields or took them from the stables. We were brought up with horses. But on the whole we Instructors of today are teaching people to understand horses as well as ride them – all at the same time. We read books and are told there is no pull or feeling of being crooked on a side saddle. No, not to us who have ridden for years but to the beginner yes, there is. While still on the ground try it by crossing right foot over your left foot while standing looking forwards, now bring your right shoulder back and feel what the beginner feels – just above your right hip bone. This keeping of the shoulders square to the front and lifting the diaphragm is the secret of straightness on a side saddle. To the beginner when she is straight she probably feels crooked. Try to help her feel the position before she moves in her lesson – but also remember you can allow people to sit on a side saddle correctly by placing their hands in such a position that holds the body in the correct position, i.e., the left hand on the top pommel and the right hand on the balance strap. This can help so very much should you have to give a Riding Club a side saddle evening, letting about twenty or thirty riders 'have a go' on a side saddle. I have done this very often using two lunge horses with two helpers lunging – this can be done in an hour and a half. The position is explained and demonstrated – questions answered, then each rider is put up, hands placed correctly – no stirrup – a walk, a trot, and a short canter – one heavyweight horse with a large saddle, one smaller horse with a medium saddle. A small saddle fits too few people to be useful. Each rider takes under five minutes.

A great many ladies who are nervous riders wish to try side saddle to see if they feel happier with their legs around a pair of pommels. Some feel they will look more attractive in a habit, with their unattractive legs hidden under the skirt. Others wish to ride their show horses in another class at the big shows. To some it is a childhood dream come true, they have always admired pictures of ladies riding side saddle and promised themselves that one day they too will ride that way. Others are disabled riders with bad hips or some injury which prevents them from riding astride; even men with only one leg have hunted side saddle, as I found mentioned in a book dated 1882, while as a child I can remember an officer who was wounded in the First World War hunting with a hook around his top pommel, his leg having been amputated above the knee. Of all the people that one is likely to teach to ride side saddle, the people who want to show their horses are the easiest because they are determined to do well and have a definite objective to work to. Small children have so much more confidence on bigger ponies and can look so attractive riding side saddle and are so much stronger on a wilful pony than when they are riding astride.

I have found teaching on the lunge so very helpful to both the beginner and the advanced rider. While the Instructor or the assistant controls the horse the rider can concentrate on her position. It is ideal for the Instructor to have someone to lunge for her, so that she can see both sides of the pupil while teaching. Keep your beginner on the right rein, because at first you must try to help your pupil to keep up onto the saddle. Working on the left rein tends to draw the weight onto the left seat bone and out of the pommels. The exercises can be learned and practised, standing still, walking, trotting, and cantering. Jumping can be started, the position held over trotting poles and cavaletti, with hands helping the position – the ideal is both hands forward on the mane, getting the folding forwards. Should the right shoulder come too far forward, then the rider is made to establish her position by holding her balance strap with her right hand – before having both hands forward – the right shoulder being the all important factor when balance is needed. The usual cry is 'right shoulder back – left shoulder forward'. Bad positioning of the right shoulder is surely the besetting sin of all side saddle riders – I do it too, as seen in some of my photographs – I look at them and think 'Heavens, look at that!'.

8
SIDE SADDLE INSTRUCTOR'S EXAMINATION AND TESTS

The Council of the Side Saddle Association decided that Instructors on the list of the Association should be competent and worthy of its recommendation. This Committee decided that Instructors should present themselves for assessment by three Examiners who would judge each candidate on her merit.

There are two grades of Instructors: B Instructors capable of demonstrating and teaching the rider up to Championship level, which in England does not include jumping, and Advanced Instructors who can teach everything including jumping and dressage up to Novice level as laid out in the FEI rules.

It was felt that all Instructors should have a good knowledge of the correct clothes to be worn by the side saddle rider and saddlery to be used, and that the B Instructors should be able to teach basic riding and demonstrate the correct position in the saddle, understand how to teach and to judge the current Equitation qualifying test for our Annual Championship show. Advanced Instructors should also be able to teach the current Championship test and jumping. The word 'current' is used as over the years both the qualifying tests and the Championship tests have from time to time been changed by the Council of the Side Saddle Association and can be found in the Side Saddle Association's year book.

The Association also runs a series of proficiency tests for the side saddle rider as set out below:

Grade One
1. Leading out in hand.
2. Knowledge of correct turn out.
3. Knowledge of the side saddle, i.e., safety stirrup and safety bar, stirrup leather and length, use of the leaping head, use of balance strap. Caring for and carrying of a side saddle.

SIDE SADDLE INSTRUCTOR'S EXAMINATION AND TESTS 49

4. Correct fitting of a snaffle bridle and correct fitting of the saddle. Prevention of sore backs.
5. Saddle up.
6. Mounting with and without assistance and with a mounting block. Dismounting with and without help.
7. Correct position in the saddle; distribution of weight; grip; normal support; reserve grip; hands, reins and stick.
8. Ride the walk, trot and canter on either rein and maintain a reasonable position.
9. Elementary knowledge of grooming, basic rules of feeding and watering a stabled and grass fed horse. Points of the horse.

Grade 2 (Must have passed Grade One)
1. Basic knowledge of aids for all simple movements.
2. Be able to ride the preliminary equitation test movements.
3. Ride in a snaffle bridle.
4. Work over trotting poles. Knowledge of the jumping position and be able to jump very small jumps up to 2' high.
5. Fit a double bridle.
6. Elementary knowledge of minor ailments.
7. Conformation of the horse.

Grade Three (Must have passed Grade Two)
1. Turn out.
2. Correct application of the aids and use of stick.
3. Correct use of spur.
4. Open and shut a gate.
5. Ability to ride at all paces over all types of terrain.
6. Jump a variety of fences up to 2' 6" high **OR** simple basic dressage movements to include 20 metre circle, rein back, lengthen strides, turn on the forehand. (Those passing both sections will receive Grade Three+).
7. Knowledge of foot care; feeding; getting a horse fit.

Grade 4 (Must have passed Grade Three)
1. He or she must be an educated rider capable of training and improving horses in their work on the flat or over fences.
2. Ability to ride and train horses to more advanced movements including: shoulder-in; counter canter; leg yielding; half pirouette; halt and lift into canter on either leg.

3. Ride the Championship Equitation Test.
4. Theory: introduce an inexperienced horse to side saddle and discuss the problems that might arise. Hereditary complaints and minor ailments.
5. Theory of equitation.

Grade Four+ (Must have passed Grades Three+ and Four)
1. Ability to ride and train horses to Side Saddle Equitation Jumping standard (3').

These Grades are open to Full members of the Association who must notify their Area Chairman when they wish to be assessed under these Grades. Grades One and Two may be taken on the same day but will be assessed separately; there must be a six month gap between taking Grades Two and Three, and Three and Four. There is also a special Junior Grade Test for those riders who are 12 and under.

Recently the Association of British Riding Schools has noted the increase in people wishing to ride side saddle effectively and have developed a series of graded tests covering both equitation and stable management as follows:

Test One
1. Discuss the history and features of varying side saddle designs.
2. Be able to recognise the three well-known makes of side saddles.
3. Tack up with a side saddle.
4. Discuss the fitting and care of a side saddle, the girths used and the prevention of sore backs.
5. Tack up with a snaffle bridle and understand its use.
6. Understand the use and fit of cavesson, drop, grakle, flash and kineton nosebands.

Test Two
1. To have passed Test One.
2. Mount and dismount from the nearside by means of a leg-up and a mounting block.
3. Check and adjust girth and balance strap mounted and dismounted.
4. Check and adjust stirrup mounted and dismounted (when

mounted the rider needs assistance in adjusting stirrup).
5. Discuss and demonstrate the correct position of the rider when using a side saddle, including distribution of weight, primary and secondary grip position of hands, reins and stick.
6. Ride from a halt to walk and walk to halt.
7. Ride a set course in walk.

Test Three
1. To have passed Tests One and Two.
2. Ride from walk to trot and trot to walk.
3. Ride a set course in trot.
4. Trot over varying terrain.
5. Show how to remove a saddle after work.
6. Demonstrate the correct use of the stick.
7. Assist a rider to mount side saddle correctly.

Test Four
1. To have passed Tests One, Two and Three.
2. Ride changes of direction and circles at trot.
3. Ride a figure of eight at trot, showing the use of diagonal lines and two 20 metre circles.
4. Demonstrate knowledge and application of the aids for the half halt, and for transitions to and from, halt, walk and trot.
5. Basic schooling over trotting poles.

Test Five
1. To have passed Tests One, Two, Three and Four.
2. Know the correct aids from trot to canter and canter to trot.
3. Ride from trot to canter and canter to trot on the right rein.
4. Ride a set course at the walk, trot and canter (on the right rein) as directed.
5. Know the sequence of the walk, trot and canter gaits.
6. Ride and maintain position at walk, trot and canter (on the right rein) without the stirrup.

Test Six
1. To have passed Tests One to Five inclusive.
2. Ride from trot to canter and canter to trot on the left rein.
3. Canter on a named leg.
4. Discuss the position of the rider when approaching and jumping fences.

5. Ride a set course at the walk, trot and canter to include two jumps of 1'6" as directed (Prix Caprilli method).
6. Demonstrate the correct use of the spur.

Test Seven
1. To have passed Tests One to Six inclusive.
2. At trot execute decreasing circles 20 metres to 10 metres and increasing circles 10 metres to 20 metres.
3. Figure of eight at canter, showing change of leg through trot on the diagonal and out of a circle.
4. Demonstrate transitions to and from an extended canter.
5. Ride at ordinary and lengthened trot and demonstrate transitions to and from each.
6. Ride and maintain position at all gaits without the stirrup.
7. Demonstrate transitions from walk to canter and halt to canter.
8. Demonstrate ability to slip and retrieve reins over fences.
9. Jump natural and coloured fences not exceeding 2'10" in height.

Test Eight
1. To have passed Tests One to Seven inclusive.
2. Be able to advise a beginner on the choice of a side saddle and of what to avoid. Demonstrate test for a broken tree.
3. Know the aids for and demonstrate turns on the forehand, shoulder in, leg yielding and rein back.
4. Ride with and demonstrate how to handle an apron whilst on the ground and mounting and dismounting.
5. Assist a rider wearing an apron to mount side saddle.
6. Demonstrate running out a horse in hand whilst wearing the apron.
7. Discuss the use of rising trot.
8. Open and shut a gate while mounted and ride a set course of five other handy pony/horse type obstacles.
9. Discuss and demonstrate how to introduce a horse to being ridden under side saddle and be able to school and improve horses in their work on the flat and over fences.

Whichever series of tests you choose, I hope that you will enjoy your side saddle riding.

9
THE REVIVAL OF SIDE SADDLE IN ENGLAND AND THE USA

In 1974 I received a letter from the newly formed Ladies' Side Saddle Association asking me to support them and I became member 23. Their aims of promoting side saddle riding and encouraging ladies to ride side saddle appealed to me, but I was surprised that anyone wanted to ride side saddle again.

Our Founders, Miss Janet MacDonald and Mrs Valerie Francis, expected to gain about 100 members, but the response was overwhelming and numbers soon exceeded this. One of the first problems was to advise members how to find suitable saddles and habits. They found an American company, Blue Riband, who were very interested and willing to back the new Association. They produced habits of all sizes and at very reasonable prices, but unfortunately the colours and textures of the habits produced were more suitable for 'fun' riding rather than what was accepted as correct dress by those riders who hunted and showed side saddle. The double Melton Cloth for making aprons was unobtainable and it was difficult to make the lighter material used hang properly.

Another problem we were all faced with was the difficulty in finding a suitable saddle. Many children wanted to ride their ponies side saddle and to find saddles for ponies was an almost impossible task. One has to realise that after about 1900 to 1905 no little girls rode side saddle until they were young ladies and then they needed a saddle of 15 inches upwards. So only the saddles of the nineteenth century were available, many of them nearly a hundred years old and many were made for donkeys. They were difficult to fit and ride on and there were really no craftsmen left by 1974 who could make them. Many saddles have been burnt as it was felt that they would never be needed again – during the Second World War many ladies gave up riding side saddle, less time and effort was needed to ride cross saddle – I burnt some myself, saddles that I bought for one pound each, how I wish I had these today!

There were few if any instructors; some of us rode side saddle but most had not studied teaching. There was Miss Sybil Smith in the south and after I became Vice-President, Mrs Francis and I visited many areas teaching and helping side saddle riders. One memorable weekend we visited Cambridge on Friday, Chichester on Saturday and then drove on to Warrington where we taught on Sunday afternoon. On Monday we were driven to Glasgow, and then I caught the midnight train home, while Mrs Francis went back to Warrington to pick up her car and drive home. Everywhere we found enthusiasm and people who really wanted to learn more about side saddle riding and the saddles themselves.

It was an uphill struggle at first but our Founders coped manfully with the National aspect. The whole of England was divided into Areas, each Area to be represented by a Chairman elected by local side saddle members and she was to sit on a National Committee. It was the duty of this person to promote side saddle in their area, persuading shows to award rosettes for side saddle riders in Open classes and to hold Equitation classes with qualifying rounds to encourage riders to compete in our National Championships. In the early days when I listened to Mr Bob Wilmer talking about an all side saddle show to be held in the future I could not envisage this being a possibility, but thanks to his drive and vision, backed by our then Chairman Miss Mackie and financed by Mrs Blois it did happen at Malvern in 1980. The very first Championship class was held at Hickstead in 1977, and for the next two years at Stoneleigh on the British Horse Society Open Day. Then we were left in a great dilemma, but Mrs Barham, Area 4's indefatigable Chairman, came to the rescue and held what is still in my mind (and I have been to every Championship held) the most pleasant and delightful Championship at Knebworth. We then had three years at the Three Counties Showground at Malvern followed by three years at Huntingdon before coming to the 1987 venue of the Newark and Notts showground. These seven shows were all side saddle shows, with classes catering for Juniors under 16 and Seniors at Novice and Open levels.

No-one has worked harder than Mrs Barham, who with her

drive and efficiency has organised three superb Display teams, first a demonstration at Wembley, then the 'Regency Ride' which was successfully taken to Denmark and Equitana Essen and the 1987 Quadrille which was also taken to Essen and was seen at both the Royal Tournament and the Horse of the Year Show.

Our Founders must be very proud of their achievements because the quality of riding both in Juniors and Seniors has improved out of all recognition. The rules for the qualifying classes have been changed from time to time but the main ideals have remained the same; that the rider and her performance should demonstrate her ability as a horsewoman to ride effectively, elegantly and of late show her ability over fences.

Having asked many questions and read books and articles written in America it appears that side saddle riding there had never really died out. Before 1900 most American ladies rode side saddle either on Western type side saddles on ranches in the cattle country, working cattle and helping their husbands, while others used the English type saddle. The side saddle developed in America in much the same way as in England, from having two pommels built up on a man's tree to being the kind of saddle manufactured by Martin & Martin in the early twentieth century. As in England riding and driving horses was a means of transport before the advent of Mr Ford and his motorcars. One reads of outstanding women who could work cattle on equal terms with men when riding side saddle or ladies such as Miss Fleitmann, later Mrs Bloodgood, who certainly hunted and competed against men show jumping before the First World War. Although children were brought up to ride astride by 1920, some girls used to amuse themselves by riding on the old side saddles in the family tack room, and a few stalwart ladies still hunted side saddle as in England, but by the 1950s side saddle riding in America seemed to be a thing of the past.

Strangely enough, in 1974, the same year as the English Ladies' Side Saddle Association was founded, the International Side Saddle Organisation, known as the ISSO, in America was started by Mrs Charlotte Kneeland who had the idea of organising those interested in side saddle and collecting knowledge and expertise. Mrs Valentine and Mrs Henderson, both well known side saddle riders in America helped with practical knowledge of how to ride and the kind of saddle to use. A small band of riders became very enthusiastic and were looking for further knowledge. By this time the ISSO were publishing a magazine *Side Saddle News* which was intended to be both instructional and social and has two most interesting regular correspondents in Mrs Jan Floyd and Mrs Clare Coley. Realising the need for further knowledge, Mrs Kneeland invited Mrs Owen over to teach and the first Clinic or Instructional Course was held. Later Miss Janet MacDonald, one of the founders of the English Association of side saddle riders, also taught in the USA. The ISSO had the greatest honour when in 1985 they provided a parade team of twenty-five for the inauguration of President Reagan.

Mrs Kneeland started to import side saddles, which in those days were mostly secondhand English saddles, then she developed her Side Saddlery business which helps side saddle riders to obtain all the necessary equipment for correct dress. A small committee was formed, rules were drawn up for certain 'divisions' of side saddle riding and there are helpful suggestions for every rider whether she be interested in parade riding, costume classes, hunting, showing, show jumping, not forgetting the very important Western section of side saddle riding with their lovely saddles, some very workmanlike as well as the most ornamental and picturesque.

When I first visited Mrs Kneeland in 1986 I was most impressed by her wonderful collection of books on side saddle, books I had never heard of mostly published in England. I spent a wonderful afternoon looking at and admiring her extensive library. But what every side saddle rider has to thank her for is her foresight in reprinting two very important books on side saddle – *The Habit and the Horse* by Mrs Clark, first published in 1857 and *Modern Side Saddle Riding* by Miss Eva Christy, published in 1909. Later I was to stay with her and teach for her.

America being such a vast country it is difficult for riders to get together and enjoy their 'aside' riding and to discuss their views and problems, so it was inevitable that small groups of riders got together and formed groups and ran instructional courses, held shows and met at local shows. One of the first things that struck me was their love of the past and I find it fascinating the way that they try to find a habit or garment of the correct period to wear when riding on an antique saddle. I have never seen so many period saddles as I did when I visited the North East Group in 1986, including some very ornate Western saddles with coloured velvet seats, ornamental stitching or silver studs.

All riders were enthusiastic, they wanted to learn, they wanted to understand more about the history of side saddle riding, to them 'aside' is the great word. We all have the same problems, the same hopes and we should all be able to draw closer together with the common aim – to enjoy Aside in America.

Side Saddle in Europe   In France there is a very active side saddle organisation run by Madame Conde. Traditional stag hunting in the forests of France has kept side saddle riders going, and recently a group of side saddle riders were instructed at Saumur on horses used at the famous French school of Equitation. The Netherlands also has a Side Saddle Association of about ten years standing.

BIBLIOGRAPHY

Anon., *The Young Lady's Equestrian Manual*, London 1838
Apsley, Lady and Lady Diana Shedden, *To Whom the Godess*, 1932, London
Beach, Belle, *Riding and Driving for Women*, New York, 1912
Bloodgood, Lida (Lida Fleitmann), *The Saddle of Queens*, Allen, London, 1959
Christy, Eva, *Modern Side Saddle Riding*, London 1907
Christy, Eva, *Cross Saddle and Side Saddle*, London 1932
Clark, Mrs Shirley, *The Habit and the Horse*, London, 1857
English, H.G., *The Art of Riding*, London, 1890
Fleitmann, Lida, *Comments on Hacks and Hunters*, New York, 1921
Greville, Lady Violet, *Ladies in the Field*, New York, 1894
Hayes, Mrs, *The Horsewoman*, London 1893
Houblon, Mrs Archer, *Side Saddle*, London, 1938
de Hurst, C., *How Women Should Ride*, New York, 1892
'Inpucuniosus', *Unasked for Advice*, London, 1887
Karr, *The American Horsewoman*, Boston, 1890
McDonald, Janet and Valerie Francis, *Riding Side Saddle*, London 1978
Mead, *Horsemanship for Women*, New York, 1887
O'Donaghue, Mrs Power, *Riding for Ladies*, London 1887
Owen, Mrs Rosamund, *The Art of Side Saddle*, Tremarton Press, 1984
Smith, Horace, *Riding Master*
Stanley, Edward, *The Young Horsewoman's Compendium*, London, 1827